A+ books

POLAR ANIMALS

NARWHALS

ARE AWESOME

by Jaclyn Jaycox

Consultant: Greg Breed
Associate Professor of Ecology
Institute of Arctic Biology
University of Alaska, Fairbanks

PEBBLE
a capstone imprint

A+ Books are published by Pebble,
1710 Roe Crest Drive, North Mankato, Minnesota 56003
www.mycapstone.com

Library of Congress Cataloging-in-Publication Data
Names: Jaycox, Jaclyn, 1983–author.
Title: Narwhals Are Awesome / by Jaclyn Jaycox.
Description: North Mankato, Minnesota: an imprint of Pebble, [2020] |
   Series: A+. Polar Animals | Audience: Age 4–8. | Audience: K to Grade 3. |
   Includes bibliographical references and index.
Identifiers: LCCN 2018056709 | ISBN 9781977108173 (hardcover) | ISBN
   9781977109972 (paperback) | ISBN 9781977108265 (ebook pdf)
Subjects: LCSH: Narwhal—Juvenile literature. | Animals—Polar
   Regions—Juvenile literature.
Classification: LCC QL737.C433 J39 2020 | DDC 599.5/43—dc23
LC record available at https://lccn.loc.gov/2018056709

Editorial Credits
Nikki Potts, editor; Kayla Rossow, designer; Morgan Walters, media researcher;
Laura Manthe, production specialist

Photo Credits
Alamy: All Canada Photos, spread 10-11, David Hosking, 8, Nature Picture Library, 19, PA Images, spread 24-25; Getty Images: Brian J. Skerry, 21, Paul Nicklen, Cover, spread 28-29; Minden Pictures: Doug Allan, spread 22-23; National Geographic: Paul Nicklen, 9; Newscom: Flip Nicklin/Minden Pictures, 5, spread 6-7, spread 12-13, 16; Shutterstock: AnnstasAg, 17, Avatar_023, 27, Dan Bach Kristensen, spread 14-15, Mara008, design element (blue), mirrelley, 17, Oliay, design element (ice window), photosoft, design element (ice), Vladimir Melnik, 26, vladsilver, bottom right 24, wildestanimal, top 11, top 15, top left 24; SuperStock: Animals Animals, 20

All internet sites appearing in back matter were available and accurate when this book was sent to press.

Note to Parents, Teachers, and Librarians

This Polar Animals book uses full-color photographs and a nonfiction format to introduce the concept of narwhals. *Narwhals Are Awesome* is designed to be read aloud to a pre-reader or to be read independently by an early reader. Photographs help listeners and early readers understand the text and concepts discussed. The book encourages further learning by including the following sections: Table of Contents, Glossary, Read More, Internet Sites, Critical Thinking Questions, and Index. Early readers may need assistance using these features.

TABLE OF CONTENTS

Unicorns of the Sea

A long tusk pops out of the icy, polar water. It's a narwhal! These whales are sometimes called the unicorns of the sea. They seem like something out of a story. But narwhals really do exist!

The Tusked Whale

Narwhals have blue-gray skin. It gets lighter as they get older. Narwhals grow up to 17 feet (5 meters) long. They weigh up to 1.5 tons. Narwhals have a thick layer of fat. It is called blubber. It keeps them warm in the cold water.

Narwhals are known for their long tusks. But a tusk is actually a tooth! It grows through a narwhal's upper lip. The tusk can be up to 9 feet (2.7 m) long.

Water flows through
holes in the tusk. These holes
help the narwhal feel the
temperature of the water.

Say "cheese"! Narwhals always look like they are smiling. They have small, curved mouths. Narwhals have tails and flippers that help them swim.

Narwhals can stay underwater for up to 25 minutes. They hold their breath. Then they come to the surface to breathe air.

Narwhals live in the Arctic Ocean. In winter, they stay in deep water. It is covered with large ice chunks. Narwhals have to swim through openings called channels.

In summer, narwhals
move closer to land and
warmer waters.

Finding Food

A hungry narwhal looks for food. Soon it spots a tasty treat!

Narwhals eat fish, shrimp, and squid. But they don't chew their food. They suck food into their mouths. They swallow it whole. *Gulp!* Narwhals get water from the food they eat.

Narwhals can dive as deep as 1 mile (1.6 kilometers) below the water's surface! They search for food near the ocean floor. Narwhals make sounds that bounce back from their prey. It tells them where their food is. This is called echolocation.

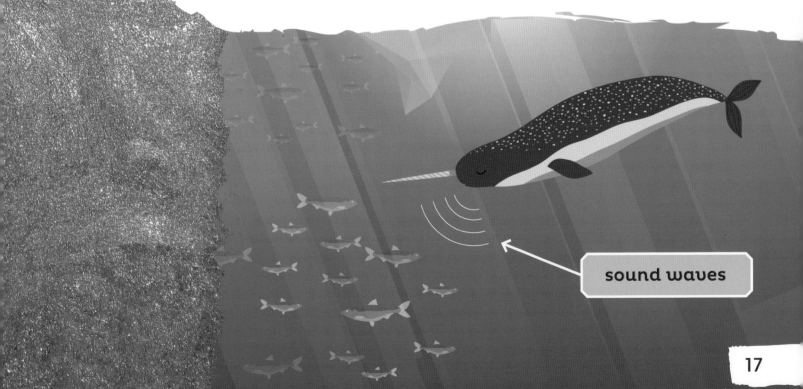

sound waves

Family Life

Narwhals live in groups called pods. A pod can have as many as 20 whales. Some pods are families. They include females and their babies. Other pods are made up of only males. They join other pods to mate. Pods talk to each other by making sounds. Narwhals click, squeak, and whistle.

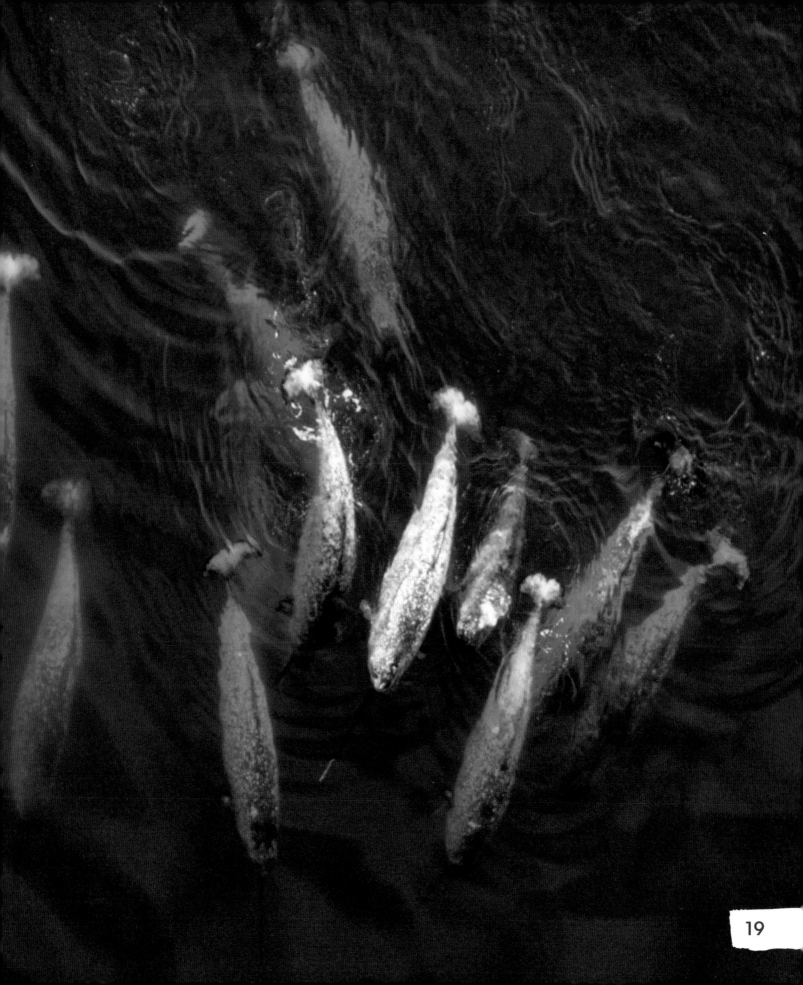

Narwhals mate in spring each year. A female has one baby at a time. The baby is called a calf.

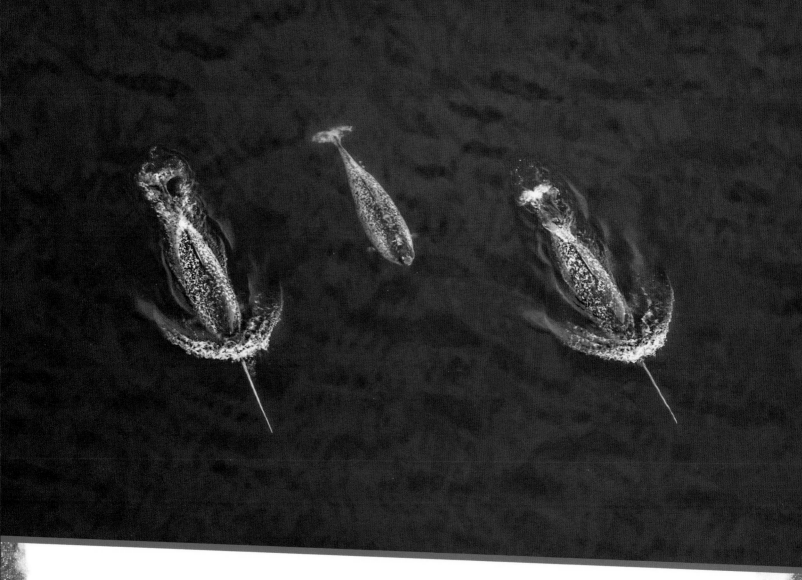

A calf is about 5 feet
(1.5 m) long. It weighs about
175 pounds (80 kilograms).
That is the size of some
adult humans!

A calf drinks milk from its mother for about 20 months. A calf learns from its pod. The pod teaches the calf how to hunt and stay safe. Narwhals can live as long as 50 years.

Staying Safe

A narwhal swims slowly. It watches for killer whales. Suddenly, it sees one. *Zoom!* The narwhal escapes. But the danger isn't gone. Polar bears and walruses hunt narwhals too.

polar bear

walruses

People also hunt narwhals. They sell their tusks or use them to make art and jewelry.

Climate change can be harmful to narwhals. Ice melts as temperatures rise. Melting ice moves while narwhals swim below. They can get trapped under ice and drown. Changes in the weather also hurt their prey. Fish may move to other areas.

About 75,000 narwhals live in the ocean. There is a lot more to learn about these awesome polar animals.

Narwhals are hard to
study because of where
they live. But they truly
are unicorns of the sea.
No other animal is quite
like them!

GLOSSARY

Arctic (ARK-tik)—the area near the North Pole; the Arctic is cold and covered with ice

blubber (BLUH-buhr)—a thick layer of fat under the skin of some animals; blubber keeps animals warm

channel (CHA-nuhl)—a narrow stretch of water

climate change (KLY-muht CHAYNJ)—a significant change in Earth's climate over a period of time

echolocation (eh-koh-loh-KAY-shuhn)—the process of using sounds and echoes to locate objects; whales and dolphins use echolocation to find food

female (FEE-male)—an animal that can give birth to young animals or lay eggs

flipper (FLIP-ur)—one of the broad, flat limbs of an ocean or freshwater animal

male (MALE)—an animal that can father young

mate (MATE)—to join together to produce young

pod (POD)—a group of certain kinds of sea creatures

polar (POH-lur)—having to do with the icy regions around the North or South Pole

prey (PRAY)—an animal hunted by another animal for food

tusk (TUHSK)—a long, pointed tooth

READ MORE

Carr, Aaron. *Narwhal.* I Am. New York: AV2 by Weigl, 2016.

Johnson, Elizabeth R. *Beluga Whales.* Sea Life. North Mankato, MN: Capstone Press, 2017.

Schuh, Mari C. *It's a Narwhal!* Polar Animals. Minneapolis: Lerner Publications, 2018.

INTERNET SITES

Kids Play and Create, Narwhal Facts
https://www.kidsplayandcreate.com/unicorns-of-the-sea-narwhal-facts-for-kids/

National Geographic Kids, Narwhals Profile
https://kids.nationalgeographic.com/animals/narwhal/#narwhal_pod.jpg

Stem Inspired Narwhal Activities
https://littlebinsforlittlehands.com/stem-narwhal-activities-ocean/

CRITICAL THINKING QUESTIONS

1. Narwhals find food in the dark ocean using echolocation. What is echolocation?
   (Hint: Use the glossary for help!)

2. How many narwhals live in the ocean?

3. How does a narwhal use its tusk?

INDEX